The Art of SLEDGING

The Art of SLEDGING

J. HAROLD

Constable • London

Constable & Robinson Ltd
3 The Lanchesters
162 Fulham Palace Road
London W6 9ER
www.constablerobinson.com

First published in Australia by Allen & Unwin, 2008
This edition first published in the UK by Constable,
an imprint of Constable & Robinson Ltd, 2009

A copy of the British Library Cataloguing in
Publication data is available from the British Library

ISBN: 978-1-84901-052-8

Printed and bound in the EU

sledging

/slɛdʒɪŋ/(*say* 'slejing')

verb **1.** *Cricket* the practice among bowlers and fielders of heaping abuse and ridicule on the person batting. **2.** *Colloquial* any ridicule or criticism. [figurative use of SLEDGE[2] + -ING[1]]

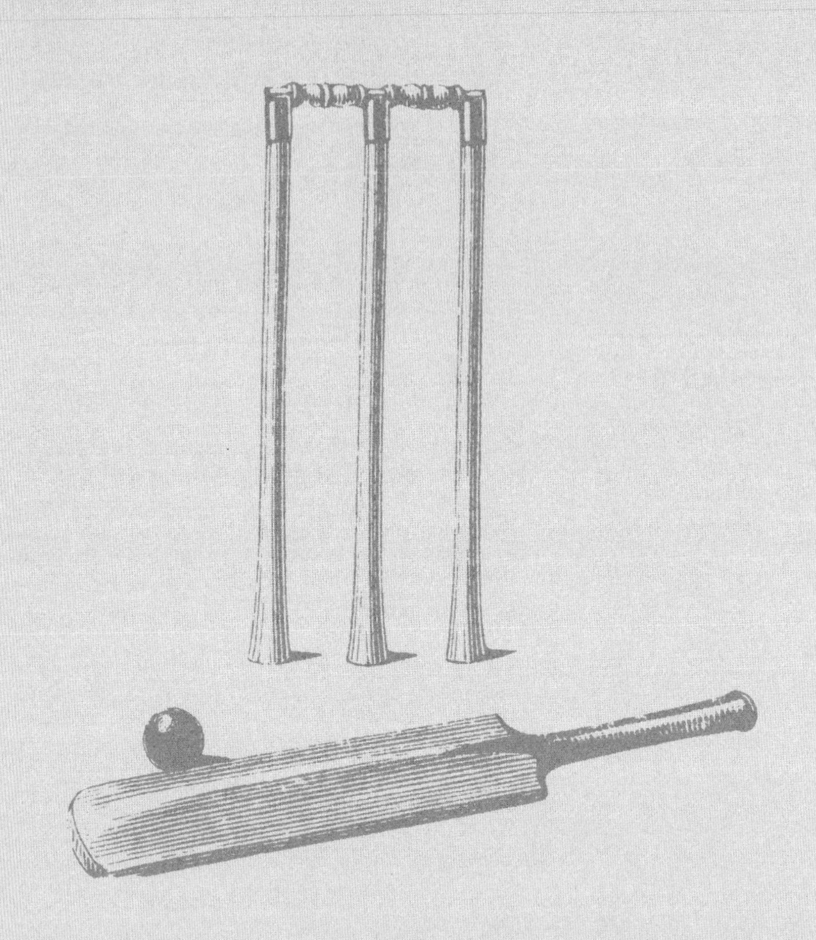

A True Gentleman's Sport

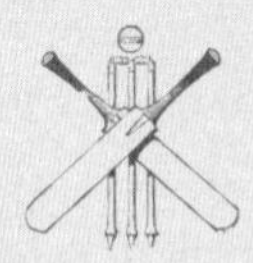

Sledging has an honourable tradition and nowhere is this tradition afforded as much respect as in the game of cricket. True, 'tis a gentleman's game and no self-respecting gentleman cricketer would be without his own personal collection of merciless remarks and cruel commentary. Fair's fair after all.

The noble art of sledging is best celebrated on the field when a lone batsmen must front eleven of his rivals and hold his own for as long, or as little, as it takes. Contact not permitted, all intimidation must be made through the brute force and fierce precision of words.

Ruthless insults and brutal replies are essential in any worthy cricket match. And it is cricket's unique pace (some call it slow) that has fostered the sledging culture. Six overs allows plenty of time for running dialogue or ongoing debate; or sometimes even a slow psychological battle of tit for tat unleashed at a tortuously steady rate.

A couple of hours facing googlies, wronguns, and wides has produced some timeless classic taunts and some brilliant comebacks.

Add to this a pitch designed specifically to be safely out of earshot of delicate ladies and it's no doubt that cricket is the true patron of the sledge.

A Bit of History

Claudius to fellow gladiator during first Olympiad at the 100-metre crease:

'Augustus! Your d*#@'s hanging out of your toga.'

CIRCUS MAXIMUS, 50 B.C.

Of course the art of sledging has been around since Roman times, but the word itself was not coined until the early 1960s. According to master sledger Ian Chappell, the use of the word 'sledge' first graced cricket vocabulary in Adelaide during the Sheffield Shield season of either 1963–4 or 1964–5, when a cricketer who swore in the presence of a lady. was considered 'as subtle as a sledgehammer'. In true Australian style, this was then abbreviated to a much more convenient one syllable – 'sledge'. The Percy Sledge number 'When a man loves a woman' was then in the top 40, so anyone swearing in front of a woman was nicknamed 'sledge' or 'Percy'. The term was soon transferred to on-field behaviour:

'There's a bit of Percy Sledge going on out there today.'

And nowhere in the world has sledging been so thoroughly mastered, finessed and crafted than in Australia.

The Science of Sledging

Although many have tried to unlock the secrets of a match-winning sledge, none have succeeded. So the search continues for the sledger's Holy Grail: the ultimate combination of words, timing, and delivery.

Only by studying history can we come to understand the true art of sledging and harness its power. Many sledges have been well documented by the players themselves or picked up by media microphones. Others have drifted through the years and become folklore.

Rules of Engagement

'Use every weapon within the rules and stretch the rules to breaking point, I say.'

FRED TRUEMAN

There are no rules to sledging – just put the other guy off his game.

The Godfather of Sledging

W.G. GRACE

18-07/1848–23/10/1915

Sporting folklore is overflowing with memorable one-liners but our search has to begin somewhere. And that place, rightfully, is with a cricket legend. Homage must be paid to the enduring wit of the great English batsman, W.G. Grace (18/07/1848 – 23/10/1915).

A champion cricketer in his own right, his remarks on the field became legendary as well. They might seem tame now, but his immortal quips played a major part in setting the standards for tone, wit and level of arrogance that today's sledger must meet. In a gentleman's game he could be anything but gentlemanly, sometimes proving that derision and intimidation can win a game. His enviably sharp and short lines, all delivered with a hidden smile, set a high standard for generations to follow.

W.G. Grace

This non-walker's stubbornness was notorious and his cockiness legendary. Once, when Grace was at the crease, the ball snuck by him and knocked off a bail. Without hesitation, he replaced the bail and told the umpire straight-faced:

'Twas the wind which took thy bail off, good sir.'

It seems Grace would only go out when he was good and ready. But the umpire gave as good as he got, humouring Grace with the famous reply:

'Indeed, and let us hope thy wind helps you back to the pavilion.'

W.G. Grace

During an exhibition match when trapped LBW by a young and unknown bowler, Grace stood motionless by his wicket and declared calmly:

'Not out. They came to watch me bat … not you bowl.'

Ironically, the best sledge involving W.G. Grace came from an opponent. Grace had dubiously managed to stay at the crease, avoiding four or five appeals. Each time, Grace had looked to the umpire to deny bowler Charles Kortright his rightful wicket. Finally Kortright knocked two stumps clean over. Grace again hesitated, waiting to be saved. Reluctantly, he finally began to walk. As he made his way past the bowler, Kortright feigned shock saying:

'Surely you're not going, doctor? There's still one stump standing!'

Glenn McGrath vs Eddo Brandes

T'was a showdown between two famous number eleven batsmen that gave birth to an all-time favourite Australian sledge. Aussie paceman Glenn McGrath was bowling to Zimbabwe's Eddo Brandes. Brandes was struggling, unable to connect with the ball but to his credit, he was valiantly protecting his stumps. A frustrated McGrath wandered up the pitch during one over and asked:

'Oi Brandes, why are you so fat?'

Quick as a flash, Brandes replied:

'Because every time I fk your wife she gives me a biscuit.'**

Even the Aussie slips fielders couldn't help but giggle. It took a few minutes before they could resume play.

Viv Richards vs Greg Thomas

This infamous exchange took place during an English county championship match between Glamorgan and Somerset in 1986. Viv Richards had uncharacteristically swung twice and missed. Glamorgan paceman Greg Thomas found the confidence to rub it in, reminding the batting hero exactly what he was trying to hit.

'It's round, red and weighs about five ounces.'

Richards hit the next ball for a clean six. He pointed the bat in the direction of the ball and said with a smile:

'You know what it looks like, now go fetch it.'

Ian Healy vs Arjuna Ranatunga

The somewhat plump Sri Lankan captain Ranatunga was at the striker's end facing Shane Warne. Warne was looking for a stumping and had tried all his usual tricks to tempt Ranatunga out of his crease, but he was having no luck. Ranatunga wouldn't budge. Constructive as ever, Ian Healy suggested from the edge of play:

'Put a Mars Bar at a good length ... that should do it.'

Kumar Sangakkara vs Harbhajan Singh

Around the time that his bowling action was reported as suspect, Sri Lanka's Kumar Sangakkara stopped Harbhajan Singh in his tracks by asking:

'So, why do you wear short sleeves when batting but long sleeves when bowling?'

Malcolm Marshall vs David Boon

Intimidating West Indian paceman Malcolm Marshall was bowling to David Boon. Boon had played and missed a couple of times. Frustrated, Marshall offered Boonie a fair ultimatum:

'Now David, are you going to get out now or am I going to have to bowl around the wicket and kill you?'

Ian Healy vs Michael Atherton

On his first tour to Australia, Michael Atherton was given a lucky reprieve when not out was called on a caught behind appeal. At the end of the day, Ian Healy walked past the lucky batsman and had a few words:

'You're a f*ing cheat.'**

To which Atherton simply replied:

'When in Rome, dear boy.'

Mark Waugh vs James Ormond

James Ormond was making his virgin walk to the pitch during the Ashes tour of 2003. He was greeted by the slightly better known Mark Waugh:

'Fk me, look who it is. Mate, what are you doing out here? There's no way you're good enough to play for England.'**

Ormond replied:

'Maybe not, but at least I'm the best player in my family.'

Paul Nixon vs Andrew Symonds

Nixon was a little-known Leicestershire wicket keeper when he was picked to tour Australia at the age of 37, a challenge he accepted with relish. Taking a leaf out of Ian Healy's book, he was a constant thorn in the Australian side with his relentless, energetic sledging. As Andrew Symonds took guard, Nixon was busy chirping away behind the stumps:

'Symo, if you edge the ball to me and I take the catch, I'm going to send you a copy of the scorecard, to your home, every day for a year.'

Craig McDermott vs Phil Tufnell

Here's a great example of how a loser can leave on top. Phil Tufnell had just dismissed Aussie fast bowler and tail-end batsman Craig McDermott, but the big redhead left him with these lasting words:

'You've got to bat on this in a minute, Tuffers. Hospital food suit you?'

Rod Marsh vs Ian Botham

When Botham took to the crease in an Ashes match, Marsh welcomed him to the wicket with the immortal words:

'So, how's your wife and my kids?'

Quick as a flash Botham replied:

'Wife's good but the kids are retarded.'

Legends of the Sledge

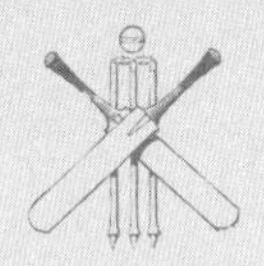

FRED TRUEMAN

06-12/1931–01/06/2006

Test Debut 1949; Tests 67

Homage must be paid to the great Yorkshire and England fast bowler Fred Trueman. 'Fiery Fred' had many classic exchanges throughout the 50s and 60s that kept the cricketing community titillated. An National Treasure, he did his country proud.

Sometimes he didn't bother trying to be witty – sheer, brutal confidence was far more intimidating. Like the time he greeted the opposing team with the fair warning:

'I need nine wickets from this match, so you buggers had better start drawing straws to see who I don't get.'

Fred Trueman

During Trueman's county career amateur cricketers, known as gentlemen, and professionals, called 'players', still competed against each other. Trueman, a proud professional, made it clear he had little time for amateurs. After humouring a young batsman, Trueman bowled him out with a beautifully crafted delivery.

The young batsman walked from the crease but not before he had the courtesy to commend Trueman's bowling prowess:

'That was a very good ball, Fred.'

Trueman replied:

'Aye, and it was wasted on you.'

Fred Trueman

In another county game Freddie was bowling to Reverend David Sheppard. Despite facing Trueman, Sheppard got a lucky 50. With a myriad of close calls, half-chances, denied LBWs, and nicks off the bat, it seemed it was the reverend's day. Trueman, being the better sport, remarked:

'Reverend, if you're as lucky on Sundays as you are on Saturdays, you'll end up Archbishop of Canterbury.'

He was just as cutting in the field. Trueman once welcomed a new Aussie batsman who went to close the gate behind him as he entered the field, with the subtle hint:

'Don't bother shutting it son, you won't be out there long enough.'

Fred Trueman

On another occasion Trueman had a batsman LBW on two consecutive balls. But both of these were denied by the umpire. Furious, Freddie reckoned he had to make his next ball count and, sure enough, with the very next ball he knocked the middle stump out of the ground. Turning to the umpire Trueman appealed, with tongue firmly in cheek:

'By gum, that must have been close!'

Fiery Fred made his name as a bowler but even with a bat in hand his wit didn't desert him. Standing at the crease and feeling the pressure, surrounded by a very close ring of Australian fieldsmen, he quipped:

'If you bastards don't back off,
I'll appeal against the light.'

Fred Trueman

No one was safe from Freddie's sardonic wit – not even his team mates. A beautiful delivery from Trueman caught the outside edge of an opponent's bat and flew directly to Raman Subba Row fielding at slip. As Trueman watched, the ball went right through the fielder's legs and to the boundary at third man. Fred didn't say a word. At the end of the over, Subba Row apologised meekly:

'Sorry Fred, I should've kept my legs together.

Trueman replied in characteristic fashion:

'Not you, son. Your mother should've!'

Aamer Sohail vs Ian Botham

In the 1980s Ian Botham returned to England from a tour of Pakistan, and, when asked to describe the country in a radio interview, joked that Pakistan is the ideal sort of country to send your mother-in-law on holiday. Needless to say the Pakistanis did not find this amusing.

So when Pakistan defeated England in the 1992 World Cup Final in Melbourne, Aamer Sohail was quick to remind Ian Botham of his comments:

'Why don't you send your mother-in-law out to play, she can't do much worse.'

Shane Watson vs Darren Gough and the ghost of Lumley Castle

While on tour in England in 2005, Queensland all-rounder Shane Watson complained of a sleepless night at Lumley Castle in Durham. Apparently the culprit was a 700-year-old ghost, which had Watson so badly spooked that he left his room to sleep on the floor of teammate Brett Lee's room.

Of course the English media and players loved the idea of the big, strapping Aussie being terrified by things going bump in the night. The next day he was greeted at the wicket by a series of spooky ghost impersonations led by English bowler Darren Gough, who was also generous enough to offer:

'Don't worry Shane, you can sleep in my bed tonight.'

Shane Watson vs Kevin Pietersen

After the ghost-busting antics at Lumley Castle, Shane Watson looked to return fire to the Englishmen. While bowling to Kevin Pietersen, Watson unloaded a tirade of sledges that, unfortunately, proved as ineffective as his bowling.

Watson's fiance, Kym Johnson, had just very publicly dumped him for her *Dancing with the Stars* partner Tom Williams. Pietersen took full advantage of this fact, replying:

**'Awww, you're just upset
cos no one loves you any more.'**

Sachin Tendulkar vs Abdul Qadir

The year was 1989, and Sachin was not even old enough to get a driving licence when he was making his debut and facing the best bowlers in the business. The Pakistani crowds jeered and mocked him, holding out placards saying, 'Hey kid, go home and drink milk.'

Facing young leg spinner Mushtaq Ahmed, Sachin hit two sixes in one over and literally sent the young bowler ducking for cover. Incensed, Ahmed's mentor Abdul Qadir came on to bowl, defending his younger team mate with:

'Why are you hitting kids? Try and hit me.'

Sachin was silent – since then we have all come to know that he lets his bat do the talking. But it didn't take him long to oblige Abdul Qadir's simple request. Sachin hit 4 sixes in the over. The over read 6, 0, 4, 6, 6, 6. David had felled Goliath ... and a legend was born.

Ravi Shastri vs Mike Whitney

Mike Whitney was twelfth man in a test match against India. He had come on to relieve an injured teammate. Ravi Shastri played the ball in Whitney's direction and looked for a single, but Whitney managed to field the ball and to rifle it back into the keeper, preventing the run.

Whitney:

'If you leave the crease
I'll break your fking head.'**

Shastri:

'If you could play as well
as you talk you wouldn't be
the fking twelfth man.'**

Steve Waugh & Ian Healy vs Nasser Hussain

With Nasser Hussain new at the crease, Aussie captain Steve Waugh looked to put the pressure on him. He directed Ricky Ponting:

**'Field at silly point.
I want you right under his nose.'**

Arch rogue Ian Healy chipped in:

**'That could be anywhere
inside a three mile radius!'**

Laughing, Nasser was out three balls later.

Mark Boucher vs Tatenda Taibu

Some sledges involve a great one-liner, others are designed to chip away at your confidence like death by a thousand cuts. During Zimbabwe's 2005 tour of South Africa, the Protea's wicket keeper Mark Boucher worked away at Zimbabwean captain Tantenda Taibu, ball by ball:

'I'm going to get you out now, because I think you might be averaging single figures this tour.'

'I'll walk you to the change rooms as well, how 'bout that?'

'What are you averaging? You must know your average ... 9 ... 10. 9 or 10?'

'I think it's 9, maybe 9.5, so we'll give you 10.'

Nasser Hussain vs Muttiah Muralitharan

1995 Boxing Day test, Melbourne. Umpire Darrell Hair controversially called Murali for a no ball for chucking, ruling his bowling action illegal. Eight years later and a continent away, Nasser Hussain allegedly welcomed him to the crease with:

'You're a f*ing cheat and a f***ing chucker.'**

Now Nasser, tell us what you really think.

Mark Waugh vs Jamie Siddons

In a Sheffield Shield game, Mark Waugh had just come into bat and was taking an eternity to take guard, asking the umpire for centre, middle and leg before stepping away towards leg side and having another look around the field, and so on.

Jamie Siddons (widely considered the best Australian batsman never to play a test match) was standing at first slip, and decided enough was enough. Finally, in frustration, he yelled out to Waugh:

'For christ sake, it's not a fking test match.'**

Waugh replied:

'Of course it isn't … You're here.'

Dennis Lillee vs multiple batsmen

Cricketing royalty Dennis Lillee had a favourite sledge that he used to great effect against a variety of beleaguered batsmen:

'I know why you're batting so badly. You've got some shit on the end of your bat.'

As the batsman examined the end of his bat, Lillee would helpfully suggest:

'Wrong end, mate.'

Legends of the Sledge

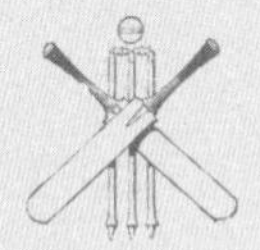

MERV HUGHES

b. 23/11/1961

Test Debut 1985; Tests 53

Merv was Australia's sledging pin-up boy throughout the 1980s and 90s. And a big boy at that. The epitome of the Aussie larrikin, he will go down in history as the cricketer who had an answer for pretty much everything. Here's a small celebration of the breadth and variety of his ... well, smart-arseness.

During the 1991 Adelaide test, Pakistani batsman Javed Miandad told the beefy Australian fast bowler that he looked like a big, fat bus conductor. When Merv claimed Miandad's wicket only a few balls later he celebrated by running past Miandad with one hand held high, yelling:

'Tickets please!'

Merv Hughes

Few cricketers can claim that they ever got the better of Sir Isaac Vivian Alexander Richards. During a test match in the West Indies, Merv didn't say a word to the Master Blaster, but continued to stare him down after each delivery, finally provoking a response from the great Antiguan batsman:

**'This is my island, my culture.
Don't you be staring at me.
In my culture we just bowl.'**

Merv didn't reply, but after he dismissed him he announced to the batsman:

'In my culture we just say fck off.'**

Merv Hughes

Merv Hughes really was one of the greatest exponents of the fine art of sledging and in one case, he even introduced a sledge that was more physical than verbal. During a tour game in South Africa, Hughes was bowling to Hansie Cronje. It was an especially flat wicket and Cronje was hitting Hughes' balls for fours and sixes all over the place. After the umpteenth boundary, Hughes headed down the pitch, stood near Cronje, let out a fart and declared:

'Try hitting that for six.'

Merv's friendly side was on display during a match against England. While bowling to Graeme Hick, who was struggling to lay a bat on anything, Hughes helpfully suggested:

'Mate, if you just turn the bat over you'll find the instructions on the other side.'

Merv Hughes

As accomplished a sledger as he was, Hughes did not have it all his own way. During a test at Lords in 1989 he was bowling to English batsman Robin Smith. Smith had played and missed more deliveries than he'd been able to hit, provoking Hughes to helpfully comment:

'You can't fking bat.'**

Simth replied, with both his bat and his words, smashing the ball to the boundary and chuckling:

**'Merv, we make a fine pair.
I can't f**king bat and
you can't f**king bowl.'**

Merv Hughes

Sometimes, Merv even copped it from the umpire. In an Ashes test match in England, he quipped to umpire Dickie Bird while bowling:

'Is that three I've had or is that three to come?'

Not to be outdone, quick as a flash Bird replied:

'Shut up, Merv, or I'll no ball you for being a smart arse!'

Freddie Flintoff vs Tino Best

West Indian Tino Best, never short of a word or two when bowling, was cleverly undone by Freddie Flintoff when he came to bat. While Best was waiting to face Ashley Giles' off spin, Flintoff quipped sarcastically:

'Watch the pavilion windows, Tino!'

The wind-up had the desired effect, causing Best to come charging out of his crease, taking a wild swing at the ball. He missed and was promptly stumped by Geraint Jones.

Not a broken window in sight.

Dennis Lillee vs Mike Gatting

No cricketer, with the possible exception of Shane Warne, has ever been as unrelentingly sledged about his weight as former England captain Mike Gatting. Stopping suddenly halfway through his run up, Dennis Lillee addressed the big man:

**'Hell, Gatt, move out of the way.
I can't see the stumps.'**

Jeff Thomson vs David Steele

Thomson made an enormous impact on the England tour of 1975, but perhaps his most lasting impression was left on silver-haired English batsman David Steele. On David's arrival at the crease at Lords, Thommo declared:

**'Who's this then?
Father F**king Christmas?'**

Bobby Simpson vs Geoffrey Boycott

Wearing glasses while batting is not ideal for any young batsmen. Unfortunately for a young Geoffrey Boycott he was one of those who did, during the 1964 Trent Bridge test. The bespectacled opener for England was greeted by Aussie captain Bobby Simpson at the crease. Simpson had the following strategic instruction for Australian fast bowler Garth McKenzie:

'Hey Garth, look at this four-eyed fker. He can't f**king bat. Knock those f**king glasses off him straight away!'**

David Hookes vs Tony Greig

If you're going to try and intimidate the opposition, it's a good idea to pick your mark carefully. Tony Greig, England's South African-born captain, greeted 21-year-old David Hookes bluntly on his debut in 1977 :

'When are your balls going to drop, sonny?'

Unfazed, Hookes replied:

'I don't know, but at least I'm playing cricket for my own country.'

He then went on to hit Greig for five consecutive boundaries.

Inzamam-ul-Haq vs Brett Lee & Brad Williams

Brett Lee is generally regarded as one of the fastest bowlers in the world but not everyone is impressed. During a particulary fast spell from Lee, batsman Inzamam pleaded:

'Stop bowling off spinners.'

Inzie must have liked the line, because he recycled it for Aussie quick Brad Williams who was bowling his heart out on a dead Pakistani track:

'I thought you would have got more turn at that pace.'

Ian Botham vs Rodney Hogg

No one could ever accuse Aussie speedster Rodney Hogg of going about his cricket half-heartedly. While bowling to Ian Botham, Hogg threw everything he had into his delivery, which caused him to overbalance in his follow-through and fall onto his knees before Botham.

It then fell to Botham to make the obvious quip:

'I know you think I'm great, Hoggy, but no need to get down on your knees.'

Allan Donald vs Allan Lamb

South African quick Allan Donald was playing in a county game for Warwickshire against Northants and was well on top of the Northants top order. Allan Lamb was on strike, looking to get onto the front foot. Noticing this, Donald dropped a couple in short to antagonise him. After the second short ball, Donald added:

'Lambie, if you want to drive, go hire a car.'

Donald pitched the next ball right up, but Lamb was ready for it and hit a beautiful cover drive straight to the boundary. He drawled:

'Go park that one.'

Amir Sohail vs Venkatesh Prasad

In the 1996 World Cup quarter final Pakistan was chasing arch rivals India's score of 287-8. Amir Sohail and Saeed Anwar went about pummeling the Indian bowling and looked set to win, reaching 110 odd for the loss of just one wicket. Sohail brought up his fifty at more than one run per ball and celebrated with a cracking four off Venkatesh Prasad. As the ball raced away to the extra-cover fence, he openly lampooned Prasad, gesturing wildly to the boundary with his bat as if to say:

'Go fetch that, Sohail'.

Trying to repeat his heroics, he was clean bowled next ball by an offering pitched on off stump. A charged-up Prasad gave him a huge send-off and the previously quiet crowd erupted with excitement. Sohail's dismissal triggered a batting collapse and India went on to claim a famous 39-run victory.

Ian Healy vs Arjuna Ranatunga

It's nice to have the odd legendary sledge caught forever on tape. This particular comment had the good fortune of being picked up by the Channel 9 microphones.

Arjuna Ranatunga called for a runner on a particularly hot night during a one-dayer in Sydney, only to hear Healy protest:

'You don't get a runner for being an overweight, unfit, fat ct.'**

Bill Woodfull vs Douglas Jardine

England's captain Douglas Jardine complained that one of the Australian players had called him a bastard. Australian captain Bill Woodfull responded by turning to his team, pointing to Jardine and asking:

'Which one of you bastards called this bastard a bastard?'

Darryl Cullinan vs Shane Warne

This is where it all began. At the Sydney one-day international between Australia and South Africa in 1997, Darryl Cullinan's somewhat tame sledging of Shane sparked their notorious long-running feud:

'Go and deflate yourself, you balloon.'

Coca-Cola

Legends of the Sledge

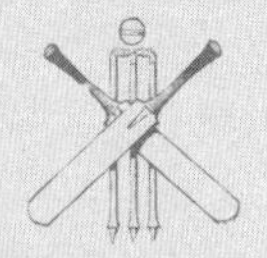

SHANE WARNE

b. 13/09/1969

Test debut 1992; Tests 145

Only someone who is mentally tough, resilient and self-assured will revel in the joys of psychological warfare. And no one loved to mess with someone else's head as much as Shane Warne. His slow bowling could be a form of torture in its own right. Add to that a narcissistic need to win and another Sledging Legend was born.

Ian Healy said of his teammate:

'Shane Warne's idea of a balanced diet is a cheeseburger in each hand.'

Shane Warne

Warnie intimidated most batsmen but the one who seemed most under his thumb was South African Darryl Cullinan. To make matters worse, Cullinan foolishly admitted he had sought a psychiatrist's help to deal with the blond spinner's mind games. When he finally arrived at the wicket, Warne couldn't wait to welcome him with the playful taunt:

'I'm going to send you straight back to the leather couch.'

Cullinan was out for a duck.

Shane Warne

Next time the two matched wits, Cullinan had the upper hand. After spending two years on the sidelines due to injury and poor form, Cullinan managed to get back into the South African test team. As he made his way to the wicket, porky Warne tried to unsettle him and play on his nervousness by chirping in his ear:

'I've been waiting two years for another chance to humiliate you.'

For once unfazed, Cullinan replied:

'Looks like you spent it eating.'

Shane Warne

Warne may not have been the wittiest sledger in the world but he was certainly one of the most effective. While bowling to a dour and watchful Sourav Ganguly, he taunted the Indian middle order batsman, saying:

'People haven't paid to watch you let balls go.'

Pointing to Sachin Tendulkar at the non-striker's end he continued:

'They've come here to watch him play shots.'

Next ball Ganguly was stumped while going for broke.

Shane Warne

After watching larger-than-life South African Brian McMillan swinging and missing at every ball he faced, Warnie just couldn't help himself, and kindly offered to tell him in advance what ball he'd be bowling.

So for the next few overs Warnie called every ball: 'leg spinner'. Next ball: 'wrong 'un'. Then 'flipper', and so it went on. McMillan couldn't lay a bat on any of them. Finally he'd had enough and walked over to Shane:

'Shane, you know you're coming to South Africa next month? Well, hundreds of people go missing in our country every day. Perhaps I'll take you shark fishing and use you as bait.'

According to former Australian captain Mark Taylor, Warnie turned white and started bowling full tosses and half-trackers.

Shane Warne

During the 2007 Ashes series at the Sydney test, the English fieldsmen, led by Paul Collingwood, decided to target Warne when he came out to bat. After copping many sledges from the Englishmen, Warnie turned to Collingwood and asked:

'You got an MBE, right?
For scoring seven at the Oval?
It's an embarrassment.'

Sledging often seems to be a case of man against man but it was a cunningly plotted and brilliantly executed team effort by Warne and Victorian wicketkeeper Darren Berry in a state match with New South Wales that caused the public breakdown of Michael Slater.

Warne and Berry had managed to get under Slater's skin by suggesting he was a time bomb just waiting to explode. They used a clever double act to ram the point home. Each time the bowler was ready to run in Berry would say:

'Tick.'

To which Warne would add:

'Tock.'

Over after over they repeated it: **'Tick … Tock. Tick …Tock.'** Slater finally got fed up, ran down the wicket and slogged the next ball up in the air and was caught. He then spun around, abusing Warne and Berry behind the wicket. Warne and Berry simply replied in unison:

'Kaboooom!'

Steve Waugh vs Herschelle Gibbs

THE MOST FAMOUS SLEDGE OF ALL

It may have the reputation as the finest sledge in modern cricket, but it seems Steve Waugh never actually said it. Rather that letting the truth get in the way of a classic sledge, sporting folklore goes like this ...

While hosting the 2003 World Cup, South Africa was facing Australia in an epic Super Six clash. The Proteas were looking for a routine victory with Australian captain Steve Waugh at the crease on 56. With the game in the balance, Waugh clipped the ball straight to South African fielder Herschelle Gibbs who, not fully in control of the ball, fumbled and dropped the ball while attempting to throw it in the air. It was a devastating cock-up.

Legend has it that Waugh took this moment to ask Gibbs:

'How does it feel to have dropped the World Cup?'

Waugh carried on to make an unbeaten 120 and Australia posted an unlikely victory, going on to win the World Cup a few days later. Waugh has, however, denied that quote. He admits he did say something to Gibbs, but claims it was more along the lines of, 'Looks like you've just dropped the match.'

Mark Waugh vs Adam Parore

Standing at second slip, the relatively unknown New Zealand batsman Adam Parore took guard at the crease, Mark Waugh watched him swing at and miss the first ball before declaring:

'Oh, I remember you from a couple of years ago in Australia. You were shit then, you're fking useless now.'**

Parore, turning around, replied:

'Yeah, that's me and when I was there you were going out with that old, ugly slut and now I hear you've married her. You dumb ct.'**

Adam Parore vs Darryl Cullinan

During a South African tour to New Zealand, wicketkeeper Adam Parore couldn't help but play on Darryl Cullinan's well-known reputation as Shane Warne's bunny. When Cullinan played and missed to New Zealand's Daniel Vettori, Parore drawled in his best Ian Healy imitation:

'Bowwwled Shane!'

Even Cullinan laughed at that one.

Kumar Sangakkara vs Shaun Pollock

South Africa hosted the 2003 World Cup and was one of the favourites to win it. But being a favourite brings with it a special kind of pressure. Sri Lankan wicketkeeper Kumar Sangakkara played on this as local hero, South African skipper Shaun Pollock, came into bat. Pollock's side needed 120 runs to win from 125 balls, so Sangakkara greeted him loudly:

'How's the pressure, skipper? He's going to let his whole country down, lads. Oh, the weight of expectations! Forty-two million people depending on Shaun.'

South Africa lost the game, were eliminated from the tournament, and Pollock resigned the captaincy.

Allan Border vs Robin Smith

Robin Smith was naive enough to ask Australia's hard-headed skipper Allan Border if he could have a drink brought out to him on the ground. Border let him know what he really thought:

**'What do you think this is?
A f**king tea party? No, you can't
have a f**king glass of water. You can
f**king wait like the rest of us.'**

Viv Richards vs Sunil Gavaskar

Batting legend Sunil Gavaskar usually opened for the Indian team, but for the 1983 test against the West Indies, he moved himself down the list to number four.

The Windies dismissed both Anshuman Gaekwad and Dilip Vengsarkar for a duck. Finally Gavaskar took his place at the crease. Viv took this opportunity to give him a match update:

'Man, it doesn't matter when you come into bat, the score is still zero.'

Gavaskar went on to score a fabulous hundred.

Paul Nixon vs Michael Clarke

During 2007 one day series, Paul Nixon, the chatty English wicketkeeper, tried to get under Michael Clarke's skin by suggesting that he had lost his good form ever since he changed the sticker on his bat:

Clarke's response:

'Nixon, you're a club cricketer, a club cricketer who's also a member of Dad's Army.'

But the English keeper accepted the challenge gleefully:

'How's it going to feel, Michael, to be caught by a club cricketer? How. Is. That. Going. To. Feel? You know what, you're going to make a club cricketer's day.'

Ian Healy vs Ben Hollioake

Another classic from master sledger Ian Healy. Ben Hollioake had just made a respectable debut. On his way back to the pavilion after finally being dismissed, Shane Warne cried out to the departing batsman:

'Hey, Ben!'

Hollioake turned round expecting a pat on the back. Instead, Healy came in from behind and said:

'Get back to the nets, you idiot.'

Steve Waugh vs Parthiv Patel

Amidst all the hype surrounding his farewell match, Steve Waugh had to contend with a dose of his own medicine from a player half his age.

As Waugh fought a grim battle to stave off defeat in the series-deciding fourth test in Sydney, the 19-year-old Indian wicketkeeper Parthiv Patel tried to unsettle the veteran batsman with some banter. The baby-faced Patel egged the 38-year-old stalwart on, urging him to try his arm one last time:

'Come on, just one more of the famous slog-sweeps before you finish.'

Waugh's reply showed he had lost none of his poise:

'Show a bit of respect, mate. You were still in nappies when I made my debut.'

Kevin Pietersen vs Chris Gayle

At the Lords test between England and the West Indies in 2007, Kevin Pietersen delivered what many believe to be the most pathetic sledge of all time to Chris Gayle:

'You're making me cross. You're making me cross. You're making me cross.'

FRIENDLY FIRE

It takes a ballsy character to sledge the opposition. But to sledge your own teammate takes a character with great set of balls.

Graham Gooch vs Mike Gatting

Despite a 79 test career, including 27 matches as captain, English batsman Mike Gatting will always be remembered for his prodigious appetite and for being dismissed by Shane Warne's first delivery in an Ashes test match. Teammate Graham Gooch summed things up with this concise sledge about the ball of the century:

'If it had been a cheese roll,
it would never have got past him.'

Allan Border vs Craig McDermott

It was during Allan Border's reign as captain that the Australian cricket team earned its current reputation for toughness – and Border earned a reputation of his own. Looking at this exchange between Border and his opening bowler Craig McDermott on a 1993 England tour, it's not hard to see why he earned the nickname Captain Grumpy:

'Hey, hey, hey, hey! I'm f*ing talking to you. Come here, come here, come here, come here … Do that again and you're on the next plane home, son … What was that? You f***ing test me and you'll see.'**

Brian Close vs Geoffrey Boycott

When it comes to dour, defensive stroke play, Geoffrey Boycott was without rival. Hence the following free-spirited advice from fellow Yorkshireman Brian Close during an English county match:

'Next bloody ball, bloody belt it or I'll wrap my bat around your bloody head.'

Chris Cowdrey and David Gower vs Mike Gatting

With friends like these ... The English captain shared this little piece of music hall comedy with his bowler Chris Cowdrey while setting the field:

Gower:

'Do you want Gatt a foot wider at slip?'

Cowdrey:

'If he gets any wider, he'll burst.'

Doug Walters vs Ashley Mallett

On tour in South Africa, Ashley Mallet was bowling to Mike Procter. As he watched Procter lustily slog his way to 50, Rowdy remembered the wise advice given to him years before: 'The only way to combat a batsman taking the long handle, is to bowl higher and shorter to him – to give him enough rope to hang himself with.'

Procter lifted Mallett's next delivery out of the ground. It landed in a brewery next door and Captain Bill Lawry wasn't risking sending any of his players to look for it. Lost ball. Undeterred and still working to his strategy, Mallett tossed the new ball up and this time Keith Stackpole got a finger to it on its way to another six.

Procter hit the third ball into the railway yards outside the ground. He lobbed the ball so high it landed in a wagon as the train pulled out of the station. The fourth went sailing into the stand and was returned, briefly, to the middle where Procter hit it again into the railway yards.

That ball didn't come back, so another new ball was tossed from the pavilion. Unfortunately for Mallett, it was collected by Dougie Walters who handed the ball to him saying:

'Well, that takes care of the reds –
now we'll start on the colours.'

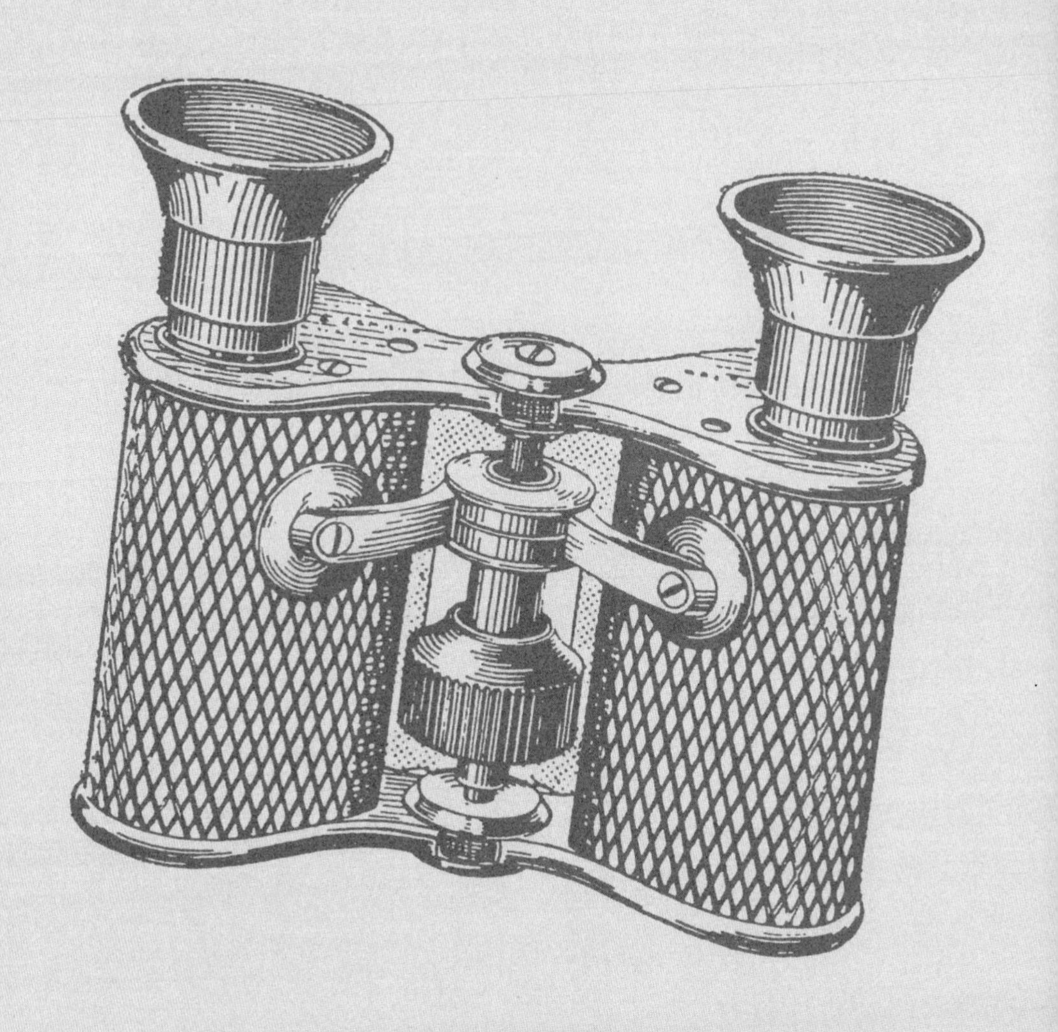

THE CROWD'S COLLECTION

Australia's cricket spectators are famously aggressive. This can, however, have the reverse of the desired effect, as South Africa's fast bowler Andre Nel once explained.

'Bring it on!' he said. 'I like to get revved up. The more people abuse me, the more I like to prove them wrong. I hope people get on my back. It will fire me up and get me going ... I carry my heart on my face when I play cricket. They call it white-line syndrome.'

Aussie crowds are only too happy to do their bit.

The Crowd vs English XI

Aussie spectator to Phil Tufnell:

**'Hey Tufnell, lend us your brain,
I'm building an idiot!'**

Spectator to an English batsman adjusting his box in between overs:

**'They're the only balls
you've touched all day!'**

The Crowd vs Australian XI

During the 1997 Boxing Day test, a run of wickets provoked a character in the crowd to helpfully suggest:

'Put Stuart Diver in – it takes 5 days to get him out!'

Matthew Hayden has copped all sorts of novel crowd barbs, including one memorable one in Sydney in 2004 which still makes him smile. Soon after the release of his cook book, Hayden walked off the SCG to the sound of:

'You are playing crap, Hayden ... and your chicken casserole tastes like shit!'

The Crowd vs West Indies

On Australia's 1973 tour of the Carribean, the West Indies were keen to introduce a young Jamaican quick named Uton Dowe, who they felt would be a suitable successor to Wes Hall. But in the first test Dowe conceded 50-odd runs from his first 6 overs to Aussie opener Keith Stackpole. Windies' captain Rohan Kanhai banished him from the attack for most of the day.

Late in the day, Kanhai decided to recall Dowe, to which a voice in the crowd responded:

'Hey Kanhai, you forgotten the eleventh commandment: Dowe shalt not bowl'!

The Crowd vs NSW Blues

In any exchange between players and members of the crowd, the crowd will always have the advantage. After all, the players have to stand there and cop it while the fans can leave whenever they like — a point echoed by New South Wales captain Simon Katich in this exchange with a fan during the Blues' Pura Cup match against the Warriors.

Fan:

'How about you play some shots.'

Katich:

'How about you go home if you don't like it.'

The Crowd vs Inzamam-ul-Haq

Pakistan were playing India in an exhibition match in Canada in 1997 when a fan called Inzamam-ul-Haq, in Hindi:

'Mota Aaloo.'

Which translates as:

'Fat Potato.'

Whatever the significance of this seemingly innoccuous insult, it provoked Inzie to rage. Armed with a bat, he spent ten minutes remonstrating with the spectator in the stands – finally being dragged away by security staff.

Silly Fat Potato.

Viv Richards vs The English Crowd

This time, one to the specatators. Viv Richards had a quick retort to racist hecklers in the crowd at Weston:

'I may be black but I know who my parents are.'

Joe the Cameraman vs Scott Muller

Who could forget Scott Muller? The Queenslander's otherwise unremarkable test debut was marred by an anonymous voice, picked up on a television effects microphone, commenting on his fielding and general ability:

'Can't bowl, can't throw!'

The notorious sledge was famously attributed to Muller's Aussie teammate Shane Warne — a charge Warne vehemently denied — provoking outrage. Eventually 'Joe the Cameraman' owned up that, in fact, he was the unwitting author of the sledge while filming the match for Channel Nine. Whether you believe Joe or not, another cricket legend was born.

Legends of the Sledge

YABBA

During the 1930s, one man dominated the hill area at the SCG in the same way that Don Bradman dominated bowlers around the world. Stephen Harold Gascoigne, better known as 'Yabba', cemented his place in Australian cricket folklore as the world's greatest barracker. He rarely missed a test or Sheffield Shield match at the SCG and, in an era when cricket was watched in near silence by the spectators, his many legendary one-liners and immortal insults could be heard clearly by players and crowd alike.

Yabba

Unpopular English Captain, Douglas Jardine, was brushing away the flies during a test match when Yabba yelled:

**'Oi Jardine, leave our flies alone,
you Pommy bastard.
They're the only friends
you've got here'**

And at the tea break:

**'Don't give the bastards a drink.
Let 'em die of thirst.'**

Yabba

Once a batsman couldn't connect with the ball, over after over. Unable to withstand this drudgery any more, Yabba yelled:

'Bowl the bastard a grand piano and see if he can play that instead!'

~

Pakistan captain Rashid Latif believed in the legacy of Yabba:

'As long as the modern-day Yabba does not use ugly language and is only sending out healthy challenges, it should be fine. In fact, it is good for the game, and adds to its competitiveness.'

~

CLASSIC SPECTATOR SIGNAGE

Richard Hadlee's much-publicised complaints about Aussie crowds in 1987 resulted in some classic banners:

'Hadlee's ego – even bigger the Ken Rutherford's nose'

'Hadlee spits the dummy'

‘Hadlee’s worse than
a whingeing Pom’

‘Even six-year-olds get
on top of Hadlee’

‘We’re sorry Mr Hawke
for calling Hadlee a wanker’

An Ashes tour tends to create a perfect storm of sledge and signage with the Aussies believing they have the edge. But the Barmy Army gives as good as it gets. A classic sign held up at The Oval during the 2005 Ashes tour read: 'You're only good at swimming'.

'If the Poms bat first, tell the taxi to wait.'

'England will win if Camilla Parker bowls.'

Ashes to ashes, dust to dust,
if Lillee doesn't get ya,
Thommo must.'

'It ain't over till
the fat man spins.'

'First the convicts, then the
rabbits and now Botham.'

BEYOND THE PITCH ...

Most sledges are excused as words exchanged in the heat of battle by those in the midst of the fray. Yet there are those cricketers who just can't resist the temptation to sledge ... from a safe distance.

Dennis Lillee vs Geoffrey Boycott

Lillee and Boycott had many classic confrontations on the field, but Lillee saved one of his best sledges for long after both their careers had finished:

'Boycott is the only fellow I've met who fell in love with himself at sixteen and has remained faithful ever since.'

Bill Lawry vs Richie Benaud

While commentating during a match in which Pakistan was faring badly in all areas of the game, Bill Lawry, offering a solution, said:

'I think Pakistan's problem is they've got to relax.'

Benaud replied nonchalantly:

'I don't agree. I think Pakistan have got to learn how to bat, bowl, and field. It's a simple game.'

Ian Chappell vs Phil Tufnell

Chappell's reputation for straight-talking didn't desert him when he moved into the commentary box:

'The other advantage England has when Phil Tufnell is bowling is that he isn't fielding.'

Martin Johnson vs Mike Gatting

Much has been written and said about Shane Warne's 'ball of the century' that dismissed Mike Gatting at Old Trafford in 1993. But Martin Johnson, writing in *The Independent*, managed to find a different angle:

'How anyone can spin a ball the width of Gatting boggles the mind.'

Richie Benaud vs Mike Gatting

Classic Richie, from 1995:

'Gatting at fine leg – that's a contradiction in terms.'

Always an impartial commentator, Benaud had just as many wry observations to share about the Australian cricket team. Pity bowler Bruce Reid …

'Well, Bruce Reid is not the worst batsman there is at international level. But those who are worse would not need to hire the Myer Music Bowl to hold a convention.'

Duncan Fletcher vs Ricky Ponting

For much of the 2005 Ashes tour, Ponting was furious at England's tactic of resting their fast bowlers while a substitute fielder replaced them on the ground. This was only made worse when Ponting was run out by English substitute Gary Pratt at Trent Bridge. Immediately after his dismissal, Ponting made his feelings clear to bemused England coach Duncan Fletcher, who later described the event:

'I smiled at Ricky Ponting. He didn't smile back. He was in a terrible temper for some reason. Quite why he was blaming me when his partner, Damien Martyn, had called him for a suicidal single to cover, I don't know. You know what's more? All the palaver caused me to burn my toast.'

Bob Willis vs Jason Gillespie

Lacking his usual zip, Aussie seam bowler Jason Gillespie copped this observation from the former English captain in 2005:

'Jason Gillespie is a 30-year-old in a 36-year-old body.'

Michael Atherton vs Merv Hughes

Former England captain Mike Atherton couldn't resist including a parting sledge at big Merv in his autobiography:

'Hughes was all bristle and bullshit and I couldn't make out what he was saying, except that every sledge ended with 'arsewipe'.'

Geoffrey Boycott vs Graham Dilley

In 1982, Boycott urged Norman Cowans (nicknamed 'Flash' as a result of being able to bowl a cricket ball at almost 100mph) to remember what happened to Graham Dilley, who started off as a genuinely quick bowler:

'They started stuffing line and length into his ear, and now he has Dennis Lillee's action with Denis Thatcher's pace.'

Matthew Hayden vs Harbhajan Singh

Early in 2008 the pair clashed during the CB Series game at the SCG when the Indians complained that Hayden had called Harbhajan a 'mad boy'. Hayden insisted he'd called him a 'bad boy' and that he should be flattered: 'It's a clothing range.'

Haydo should have left it there but speaking on a Brisbane radio station, he couldn't resist adding:

'It's been a bit of a long battle with Harbhajan. The first time I ever met him he was the same little obnoxious weed that he is now.'

Douglas Jardine vs All Australians

England's captain, Douglas Jardine, is known in sporting lore as priggish, ruthless and a hater of Australians:

'All Australians are an uneducated and unruly mob.'

Remember …

{ to offend is to win }

… so do your bit to protect Australia's sledging edge

Try using these one-liners at your local cricket pitch:

'Keep batting like that and you'll grow some tits.'

'He does know it's the f**king mown strip right?'

'You bowl like f**king Tufnell.'

'No one told me we were playing the special school today.'

'I've seen more pies today than
I would at a bake-off.'

'This bloke can't bowl a hoop down a hill.'

'Big swing, no ding.'

'Ring your mummy – tell her
you'll be home before tea.'

'If that was a doughnut,
you wouldn't have missed.'

'So, what does your boyfriend do
while you play cricket?'

'You are not a batsman's arsehole.'

3 minutes later:

'Sorry, I stand corrected.'

'You couldn't hit the water
if you fell out of a boat!'

'Easy wicket here boys, he's sweating
more than a pedophile at a Wiggles concert.'

For when number three walks to the crease:

'Into the tail now, lads!'

'More blocks than a Lego set.'

'What's your hurry fat boy?
Krispy Kreme is open to midnight.'

'You've got him fishing like a garden gnome.'

'I've seen better batting in the shower.'

'I've seen a better batter in a fish shop.'

'Oh dear, someone go get
the tennis ball from the car.'

'This guy's made more runs on the toilet.'

'Hang on boys cos this guy can't drive.'

'This guy doesn't have a girlfriend
cos he can't pull.'

'What are you going to do
after I've warmed up?'

'More swings than a playground.'

'Oi … you're too fat for batting …
… but we need a new roller.'

'Come on boys, he's number
(9-11) for a reason.'

'Are you much of golfer yourself?'

'He's swinging like a monkey on steroids.'

'He's swinging like the '60s.'

'Shouldn't having four eyes
give you better vision?'

'Ooooh he swings both ways.'

'More nicks than a Greek wedding.'

'Better ease off a bit,
this one's still on the tit.'

'A lot of helmets here boys,
you must be scared.'

‘When’s the game itself going to begin?’

Groucho Marx watching a match at Lords

Picture Credits

Page 18: Fred Trueman, courtesy Getty Images. July 1963. Fred Trueman, England fast bowler, who played for England in 67 Test matches between 1952–1965. Credit: Popperfoto.com

Page 34: Merv Hughes, courtesy Newspix. December 2, 1988. Australia's Merv Hughes celebrates after dismissing Desmond Haynes in the second test against West Indies at the WACA in Perth. Photographer: News Ltd.

Page 52: Shane Warne, courtesy Newspix. March 14, 2000, first Test, Australia v New Zealand at Eden Park, Auckland. Shane Warne celebrates equalling Dennis Lillee's Australian Test record of 355 wickets after he bowled Nathan Astle. Photographer: Phil Hillyard.